The
SECRET FORMULA
to be
FREE
of DEBT

Richard King

iUniverse, Inc.
New York   Bloomington

The Secret Formula to be Free of Debt

The information, ideas, and suggestions in this book are not intended to render professional advice. Before following any suggestions contained in this book, you should consult your personal accountant or other financial advisor. Neither the author nor the publisher shall be liable or responsible for any loss or damage allegedly arising as a consequence of your use or application of any information or suggestions in this book.

iUniverse books may be ordered through booksellers or by contacting:

iUniverse
1663 Liberty Drive
Bloomington, IN 47403
www.iuniverse.com
1-800-Authors (1-800-288-4677)

Because of the dynamic nature of the Internet, any Web addresses or links contained in this book may have changed since publication and may no longer be valid. The views expressed in this work are solely those of the author and do not necessarily reflect the views of the publisher, and the publisher hereby disclaims any responsibility for them.

ISBN: 978-1-4401-7752-1 (pbk)
ISBN: 978-1-4401-7753-8 (ebk)

Printed in the United States of America

iUniverse rev. date: 1/11/2010

Acknowledgments

Many people contributed to the writing of this this book in a multitude of ways, both large and small. First and foremost I thank Val Anderson , she is the most increble person that I ever know a great friend, and she also proved to me that even that she is my ex wife, she can be my best friend, she supports my idea to write this book all the way from the beginning to the end ! My friend Bill Grainger his generosity and kindness it is something that I have no word do express my gratitude. Thanks also to Open vision staff, they design the site that I ever see ! I finally , I'd like to thank all my clients from www.4001kcapitalmanagement.com for showing me how to help them to be debt free.

Now I would like to invade you to visit me at
http://mrrichardking.blogspot.com/

This is my blog and I love to get messages and exchange ideas. www.facebook.com/mrrichardking

Here I keep all my friends inform about the news stock market, and also it is a great place to know you better.
www.twitter.com/MrRichardking

Follow me here and you will know where I am We go in churches ,school , univerty so will be great if you follow me and meet me.

Thanks and enjoy !

Word From Richard King:

Are you ready to learn the most powerful formula to be debt free and live the life that you always dreamed of?

You are about to know how you can turn your life around, just like thousands of my clients did.

I saw them turn their debt into prosperity and a wealthy l. Now they are living a happy life. Anyone can do it – even a baby can. How?

By reading this book, following its principles and implementing them. It is really that easy. Make no mistake. This information is powerful and will change your life and habits. The secret that will reset your mind and bring you happiness is revealed.

This is not some wild claim to get you to buy this book. These are time tested principles and a secret formula to help you and your family to change directions. No more stress, no more collection calls, no more checking the caller ID before picking up the phone. You will change your life and see the happiness come back into your life. Don't forget that you will learn how to save more, make more money, build your **factor prosperity** and of course how to be debt free.

Keep reading!

Good luck, God bless you !

And thanks for investing in yourself – the most valuable investment you can make!

Introduction

Dear Friend,

Congratulations!

By making the decision to purchase **The Secret Formula to be Free of Debt**, you have taken a phenomenal step towards a level of prosperity and financial independence. Within the pages that follow you will find all the information you need to get completely out of debt including your home mortgage and will ultimately be living comfortably off your investments without fear or stress. That may sound like a dream, but this dream is going to come true for you.

Before we start, let me explain to you how this secret formula works. First, everything that you want in your life you need to put extreme good energy and here is nothing different. Maybe now I am revealing to you the real secret of this program. Set your mind right now. Develop a confident mind and make the commitment. It may seem a bit silly to you, but declaring that you are seriously committed to complete this secret formula may be the most important step toward achieving personal wealth. You are standing here and now and now getting yourself out of debt and becoming financially free is a serious goal to you. More than that it is a goal that you are passionate about. So now just repeat to yourself as a simple exercise, "I will be free of debt, no more fear, no more stress, never again will I be in this situation."

Having said that, let me start to introduce to you what you will need to succeed and what you will achieve. You will need **time**, **discipline** and **honesty**. **Time**, because in order to achieve the success using this formula, you need to dedicate time. It takes time to work through the components of this formula. It takes time to learn a new mindset and ways to save money in your unique life. It takes time to decide how you want to invest. It is probably not a surprise to you that you need to be **disciplined**, but don't worry – if you don't have self-discipline now, by the time you complete this formula, you will have the motivation and tools that you need to get debt free and stay that way. You need to stick with the formula. It is a proven system. Just follow it! **Honesty** is also needed. Honesty with yourself is taking a deep look inside yourself and your situation. Do this will allow you to apply the secret formula to make the necessary change and achieve success and a debt free life.

What will you achieve?

I don't care who you are, how much money you make or if your credit card is maxed out and you have a huge mortgage to pay off. You will pay off all your credit cards. You will pay off you car, and you will pay off your mortgage in no time. We will divide our secret formula into four parts. **Part one is Take Action**. In this section you will be introduced to the secret formula, how it works and how long it will take you to be free of debt. **Part Two is Twenty Tips to Never Be in Debt Again and build Prosperity.** This section is where you become aware of all mistakes that you have made and that you can never make again. You will remain focused on developing prosperity. You will be encouraged to become educated and get more knowledge. With additional knowledge, you will be able to protect yourself to avoid repeating previous mistakes. **Part three, Meat and Potatoes**. This is my favorite part because once you are free of debt and using the Fifty Steps to avoid returning from where you were, we will give you steps to build wealth and finally achieve your financial freedom. In **Part four, Bibliography of The Secret Formula to Be Free of Debt.** Now we are ready to get started!

PART 1

Take Action

If you can't make yourself do things that could improve your life, your life will likely end up right alongside the other 95% of the financial failures in America. It's that simple. You can have the best opportunity, the best plans and the best tools, but if you can't pull all of that into action, it's all a waste.

You must find in yourself the resolve to ACT! Otherwise your thinking won't amount to anything. Some of the world's greatest failures died thinking about what they were going to do.

Don't forget what I said, "Discipline, Time and Honesty." You will need all of these elements right now. Don't wait. Don't wait until the next bill or the next fight with your family. It's now or never. Take action. Do it. I believe it was Tony Robbins that said that out of pain and desperation comes inspiration. Let's go and find your inspiration together.

Where Am I Going to Start?

You are confused. Maybe nervous and disorganized and have no idea what to do. Where are you going to start? All right, take a deep breath and think for a moment that you are a company. Yes, let's say you are a big company whose balance sheet does not look good right now. Your company needs a new CEO, new mentality and new attitude. You are the new CEO. You are the one that will turn things around. What to do now? As the new CEO of your life you are going to start organizing yourself. Get every credit card statement, mortgage, insurance bills, everything that you can possibly think of. Remember what I told you about the three elements? You will need time. I recommend you start on the weekend or a day off. Why? You will feel the pain and of course, you are in debt now, but feel the pleasure of taking this matter into your hands. You will be debt free in no time. Having said that, what are you waiting for? Get all you need now. Go and find at least the last three months of all of your debt and let's start to reorganize your life.

Analyze Your Own Balance Sheet

Did you get everything? Did you get the bank statements for all of your bank accounts? Everything? We need to discuss the problems that you, as the new CEO of your company need to know about. First, do you know the difference between debt and expenses? No? It's very simple. Debt is everything that you can pay off such as credit card debt, car, and mortgage. Expenses are your utilities, insurance, taxes and the things that even when you have plenty of money and are debt free, you will still have to pay. It is important to know that because you are the new CEO and you must know how to deal with all of these things. Besides, it is important to know that how big your problem is. Now you are probably asking yourself, do I need to know all of that? Is it going to help me? Yes, it will, as a matter of fact as the CEO this is how you can start to change the balance sheet of your company. Note that you know have everything a bit more organized. You are close to see how your company, (your life) is doing. You can now see how the ex-CEO, the old you, wasn't doing a very good job. I have prepared for you several balance sheets that are going to help you to have a close view of the real situation. Choose one and fill it out. Choose whichever one you prefer, but take a look at the last one. I call this one, "Reducing your monthly expenses." I want you to fill this one out, no matter which balance sheet you choose. I don't have to remind you that you are in debt. Find a way to save a little and make that part of your new mentality and attitude. Now comes the discipline. You must be honest. You, and only you can change your balance sheet from a negative to a positive, get out of debt and turn this situation around. Again, pick up the balance sheet, fill it out and keep my favorite in mind. Start to dig into your mind and habits to see what you can do to save a little bit more. Go on and fill those out.

Ways to Save

Now you have learned a lot. You are organized, and have learned about debt and expenses. Now we will introduce the **FP – The Factor Prosperity**. First we must show you a couple of ways to save money. You will learn how to build your FP. To do this – we need to know where your money is going. Once again, we need to be disciplined. I am not going to ask you to cut up your credit cards, but will ask you to not create any more debt. You can't afford to create additional debt. Take all of your credit cards away from yourself. This is not a negotiable policy – you just need to do it. Again – discipline is crucial here. Remember, you are reading this book, you have invested in this formula and you want to be free. Now every time that you think about buying something, step back and think about your commitment and your goals. If you do this right away, you will switch your mindset. You will not step away from your plan. Here I want to introduce to you some ideas to save money and put that money back into your FP and to work for you. I know that you are asking, "What is FP?" Hang in there and hold on – we will get there soon. Here is how to save some money on a daily basis.

Insurance (car) – Do you know that you can raise your deductible and reduce your premium right away?

Groceries – Most people spend $500 or more a month on groceries, but using discount coupons and shopping sales can save you at least 10% on your grocery bill. That's $50-$100 per month that can be added to your FP.

Eating out – Just going out to lunch each work day instead of bringing something from home can easily cost you $100 per month. That's an additional $100 that could be included in your FP.

Movies – We have become a nation that feels deprived if we don't go to the movies or watch a Pay-per-View. A movie and pizza for two can cost you another $100 from your budget. If you can find alternatives that are free or inexpensive that would be another $100 for your FP.

Feeding the kids – Fast food chains have made fortunes convincing American parents that their children can't leave without special, fun meals and the toys associated with them. Incessant Saturday morning television commercials compound the problem. The point is that taking the kids out to lunch or dinner once or twice a week can cost a lot of FP dollars.

Maybe you could think of satisfying snacks and meals that could be made at home. If the kids complain, remember you are the big person, and they are the little person.

Extended Warranties - In case you have to buy and only if you HAVE to buy a big-ticket item, never get the extended warranty. Like most other forms of insurance, extended warranties are most likely never going to be needed by the person purchasing them. With most modern products, if they are going to break down, they will within the initial, FREE, manufacturer's warranty period. If it was likely that your car stereo, washer, microwave or television would have the troubles covered by an extended warranty, they would not sell the warrantee to you. But sell they do and sometimes vigorously because there are a lot of additional profits in extended warranties.

With these ideas alone, we have found several hundred dollars alone for your FP. I bet you can think of more. Especially now that you have seen how much difference they can make on a daily basis. Remember our goal here is to find a leak. Yes, just like a plumber that goes into your house to fix a leaking problem, this is the perfect example to think about. Your water bill goes up and you don't even know why. So, your plumber finds what's wrong, fixes it and your water bills go down. That's the idea here. I am not saying that you can't go to a movie or buy a gift for your wife on her birthday, don't be to hard on yourself, but be honest. Reward yourself. Let's say you paid your first debt off. You are allowed to celebrate. Sure – go ahead. Why not? In the end, you are the CEO – you know what is best, when and how to spend the money is important. This is about being happy, wealthy and debt free.

We want to give you room to enjoy yourself, but don't lose your focus on the goal.

The Factor Prosperity

The Formula is Revealed

Let's discover the power of FP. This is the engine that makes this vehicle work. You are about to see for yourself that it is really possible to become totally debt free.

The plan:

1 – Prioritize your debt (using the formula you will be given here).
2 – Make the minimum required monthly payments on all debt, except the highest priority debt.
3 – Add the whole FP to the regular payment on the highest priority debt. (We will cover the FP in detail) For now assume an amount equal to 10% of your take home monthly income.
4 – Continue doing this each month until that debt is paid off.
5 – Then when the debt is paid off, move on to the second debt on your priority list. You will now have an even bigger FP than before because you can the amount you were paying on the initial debt to this monthly payment.
6 – Repeat again and again, as you move down your debt priority list.
7 – On average, people pay off all of their credit cards and their car within the first couple of years. After that they are typically able to double their monthly mortgage payment. Within four to five years, the mortgage is burning in the fireplace and they are completely debt free.

Can you imagine that? You could own your car, your house, and be completely debt free within five to seven years. Let's work this using some numbers. On the worksheet, you will have an opportunity to use your own numbers, but for now, let's make up an easy to follow scenario. To start, say you have a $100,000 mortgage and that your payments are $734.73/month. After you've paid off all of your other debt, we will say you now have a $2061 Factor Prosperity to apply to your mortgage. That means you will now be paying $2794.73 on a $100,000 mortgage. Do the math. You will be paid off in 35 months. That's just 4 years and 4 months. Of course, we neglect the effect of interest here. That would extend the payoff by a few months, but even if it turns out to be eight months, you are still going to be paid off in just five years.

Your next-door neighbor who has the same mortgage and pays only $734 per month will still have 26 years left on his mortgage when yours is gone. Even after 24 years of paying his mortgage, he will only have paid off a little more than half of the principle. You, on the other hand, will be investing your $2794.73 a month for the 26 years it will take your neighbor to pay off his mortgage. He will have a house. You will have a house and a debt free and prosperous life.

To get a rough idea of how long it will take you to get completely free of debt, including your mortgage. We will use the FP Time Calculator on the next page. First, total up all of your debt balance. This number should include your mortgage balance and will be an impressive amount. However, you will be encouraged when you see what happens as we short circuit the vast impact of compound interest working against you. By paying these bills off using the shortest mathematical route, you will see results instantaneously.

Locate your approximate total amount of debt in the total debt amount column along the left edge of the FP Time Calculator Chart. Then run your fingers across to the right until you reach your approximate total monthly amount available for payments on all of your bills. Include your mortgage in this amount. This income amount should include both of your FP and the normal minimum monthly payments on all of your bills. Do not include the money that will go towards your non-debt monthly expenses such as food, utilities, gasoline and insurance.

When you locate this monthly amount, follow that column up to the line at the top of the table and you will see the approximate number of years it will take you to get completely out of debt. This chart will show you why you will want to put the most you can into your monthly pay-off FP. The lower the monthly amount you can muster against your total debt load, the longer it will take you to pay it off. The longer the pay off takes, the greater the portion of your money that will be going towards interest versus lowering the principle.

Let's see an example of how paying off debt might work. If your debt including your mortgage totals $200,000 and the total monthly income (include your FP) you had for payment on your debt was $4100, you would first locate $200,000 in the far left column, then look across to the right and find $4152. This is the amount closest to the $4100 you have available each month. Then run your finger up to the top of the column and you will see that it will take 4 years to be paid off. All of your debt, including your mortgage would be paid off in just 5 years.

Be honest with yourself. What plan do you currently have or have you ever heard about that could get you totally debt free in that short time? To get a handle on how brief that time is, simply think back five years. Doesn't' it seem like just yesterday? Well, that's how quickly you will be looking back and remembering how hard it was carrying your heavy debt on your back. Another feeling you will have is complete freedom and you will never be that vulnerable again. That is not to say you will necessarily quit your job or radically change your life when you are debt free. You might, but you might not. The point is for the first time in your life you will be in a position to make that choice. Once you are debt free, even before you've started your investments, not boss will be able to hold your job over your head again. You will be able to survive without it. You could easily live on unemployment or savings until you found other work. Or maybe you would just choose to move to a less expensive area and start a home-based business. The important thing is that the immediate pressure would be off and you would have options. Think about how many people spend everyday wishing that they had a plan B, worrying about the economic situation or their company's stability. According to a recent NBC television report, America has lost 32 percent of its jobs in just the last ten years and it is still losing 2500 jobs everyday. Once you begin building your investment portfolio, which starts happening the month after your last debt is gone, you will quickly build up more than sufficient emergency reserves. After just a few months, you will have as much in the bank as any credit card would ever offer you as a credit line. So you can be your own credit card, or bank from that moment on. By the end of the first year, you will have more in your savings and investments than you will probably dare to dream right now. We will talk more about your investments in Part 3- Meat and Potatoes.

Total Debt Amount	1 year	2 years	3 years	4 years	5 years	6 years	7 years	8 years	9 years	10 years
$ 1,000	$ 87	$ 46	$ 32	$ 25	$ 21	$ 18	$ 16	$ 15	$ 14	$ 13
3,000	262	137	95	75	62	54	48	44	41	38
5,000	437	228	159	124	104	90	80	73	68	63
7,000	612	320	223	174	145	126	113	103	95	89
10,000	875	457	318	249	208	180	161	147	135	127
15,000	1,312	685	477	373	311	270	241	220	203	190
20,000	1,749	914	636	498	415	361	322	293	271	253
30,000	2,624	1,371	954	747	623	541	483	440	406	380
40,000	3,498	1,827	1,272	995	830	721	644	586	542	507
50,000	4,373	2,284	1,590	1,244	1,038	901	804	733	677	633
75,000	6,559	3,426	2,385	1,866	1,557	1,352	1,207	1,099	1,016	950
100,000	8,745	4,568	3,180	2,489	2,076	1,803	1,609	1,465	1,354	1,267
125,000	10,931	5,711	3,975	3,111	2,595	2,253	2,011	1,831	1,693	1,583
150,000	13,118	6,853	4,770	3,733	3,114	2,704	2,413	2,198	2,031	1,900
200,000	17,490	9,137	6,360	4,977	4,152	3,605	3,218	2,930	2,709	2,534
250,000	21,863	11,421	7,950	6,221	5,190	4,506	4,022	3,663	3,386	3,167
300,000	26,235	13,705	9,540	7,466	6,228	5,408	4,827	4,395	4,063	3,800
350,000	30,608	15,990	11,130	8,710	7,265	6,309	5,631	5,128	4,740	4,343
400,000	34,981	18,274	12,720	9,954	8,303	7,210	6,436	5,860	5,417	5,067
450,000	39,353	20,558	14,310	11,198	9,341	8,111	7,240	6,593	6,094	5,700
500,000	43,726	22,842	15,900	12,443	10,379	9,013	8,045	7,325	6,771	6,334
550,000	48,098	25,127	17,490	13,687	11,417	9,914	8,849	8,058	7,449	6,967
600,000	52,471	27,411	19,080	14,931	12,455	10,815	9,653	8,790	8,126	7,601
650,000	56,843	29,695	20,670	16,175	13,493	11,717	10,458	9,523	8,803	8,234
700,000	61,216	31,979	22,260	17,420	14,531	12,618	11,262	10,285	9,480	8,867
750,000	65,589	34,264	23,850	18,664	15,569	13,519	12,067	10,988	10,157	9,501
800,000	69,961	36,548	25,440	19,908	16,607	14,420	12,871	11,720	10,834	10,134
850,000	74,334	38,832	27,030	21,152	17,645	15,322	13,676	12,453	11,511	10,767
900,000	78,706	41,116	28,620	22,397	18,683	16,223	14,480	13,185	12,189	11,401
950,000	83,079	43,401	30,210	23,641	19,720	17,124	15,285	13,918	12,866	12,034
1,000,000	87,451	45,685	31,800	24,885	20,758	18,026	16,089	14,650	13,543	12,668

Total Monthly Accelerated Payment Amount

Your Factor Prosperity

I've thrown this term Factor Prosperity and you are probably wondering, "What is it? What part does it play in the debt payoff process?" The best way to describe how FP works is to think about rolling a snowball downhill to build your snowperson. As you roll, it picks up snow, grows larger and builds momentum. The snowball in my system is what I call Factor Prosperity. I am going to help you put together your FP in the next page but for now I want you to understand that this is the money that will drastically accelerate the payoff of each debt. The reason I am showing you how the FP works in my system before I actually help you put it together is because I want you to be fully motivated to pursue every dime of potential FP money before I show you where to look for it. If I had explained where your FP money might come from before you saw how powerful each FP dollar could be in paying off your debt, it would have simply been an academic exercise. But once you see how quickly the FP can help melt away debt, you will be thinking up your own ways to add dollars to the process.

I recommend you use 10 percent of your monthly net income for your FP. This will be a workable number for the calculations. It will give you an understanding of how the FP works and a frame of reference for what could be accomplished by the FP.

Let's get down to paying off your debt

Definition: for the purpose of this formula – a debt is an amount that can be completely paid off. Ongoing costs such as food, taxes or utilities are expenses. True – you want to minimize them, but they are not to be included in our formula because they can never be paid off. We already talk about that but at this point it is just not bad to remind you what is debt and what is expenses. Got it ?

Let's get started.

As we explained before and I hope you have already all of your debt written down, now you will start to use the DEBT FREE FORM to help you to calculate when you will be debt free. Let's say you have a Visa card with a $500 balance and a minimum monthly payment of $25, you would divide $500 by $25 and get an answer of 20. This doesn't mean anything in and of itself, but it is the first step in determining the proper order in which to pay off all of your bills. Do for each bill and record the answer to each division in the appropriate column on your DEBT FREE Form. Next, starting with the lowest division answer – number the bills from 1 to whatever number of bills you have to pay off. Put this number in the payoff priority column. For example, if you had two bills (Visa and a department store charge) and the Visa division gave you the answer of 20 and the department store came at 17, the department store account would be priority number one and the Visa would be number two.) This number indicates the order in which you should pay off your debt. You would pay off the department store first and the Visa second. If two or more debts come out with the same answer, prioritize the debt with the lower balance to be paid off before the debt with the higher balance. It is not important which account has the highest interest rate because this formulate accelerates the payoff so that you will not be paying enough months of interest for it to make a significant difference. You are going to beat your creditors at their interest game and turn off the flow of money they have been taking out of your financial life.

Analyze how the debt was prioritized on the sample calculating your DEBT FREE FORM. Note how their FACTOR PROSPERTY(FP) was added to the first debt then how their increased FP was cascaded down to the second debt, the third debt and so on. Take a look !

Factor Prosperity

-SAMPLE-

A. Write down your factor prosperity at right. _____ $400

B. Try for 10 percent or more of your monthly take-home income.

C. Write down each debt name in the first column below, its total balance in column 2, and its minimum monthly payment (excluding tax, insurance, or any amount you might typically add to it) in column 3.

D. Divide the total balance of each debt by its monthly payment, and put the answer in column 4.

E. Prioritize your debts in column 5, beginning with the debt with the lowest division answer as priority debt #1, the next lowest division answer as priority debt #2, and so on.
Column 6 is where you add your Accelerator Margin (from A. above) to the monthly payment amount for priority debt #1 and put this total to the right under Accelerated Monthly Payment. Now divide debt #1's Total Balance by this Accelerated Monthly Payment. The answer goes in column 7.

F. When debt #1 is paid off, take its Accelerated Monthly Payment (which contains the original Accelerator Margin and debt #1's monthly payment) and add this amount to the monthly payment on debt #2. Put this new monthly payment in column 6 as debt #2's Accelerated Monthly Payment.

G. Continue adding each paid-off debt's Accelerated Monthly Payment to the priority payment of the next priority debt to accelerate its payoff — until you've eliminated all your debts.

Name of Debts 1	Total Balance 2	Monthly Payments 3	Division Answer 4	Payoff Priority 5	Accelerated Monthly Payments 6	Months to Pay Off 7
Mortgage	100,000.00	788.00	1.06	5	2,798.74	36
MasterCard 1	1,700.00	34.00	50	6	1,678.54	2
MasterCard 2	3,287.00	65.74	50	7	1,792.28	2
Visa	1,550.00	31.00	50	5	1,644.54	1
Discover	850.00	17.00	50	4	1,613.54	1
Department Store	2,122.00	63.66	33	3	1,596.54	2
Car 1	12,350.00	672.90	18	2	1,582.98	8
Car 2	7,250.00	592.08	15	1	891.08	9
Home Equity Loan	23,930.00	316.69	84	8	2,860.97	12
TOTALS	**$152,639.00**	**2,394.89**				**72**

H. Total Debts (total column 2): $ 152,639.00

I. Total Monthly Payments (total column 3): $ 2,394.89

J. Total Accelerated Payments (A + I): $ ($400-2,394.83) = 2,794.83

K. Years to debt-freedom (total column 7 ÷ 12): (72÷12) = 6 years

19

The Power of the Factor Prosperty

Now it is time to start rolling the bills' payoff and letting it snowball down hill. During this process you will be focusing all of your FP on one debt at a time, putting minimum allowed payments on all other debt. On the sample form you will see the $400 FP at the top of the DEBT FREE FORM, add that $400 to the regular payment for the first debt to be paid off. Now, simply divide the total balance on this loan ($7,260) by the FP monthly payment amount of $891.08. (The regular monthly payment plus the FP) Being paid on the car loan each month, you can see that it will now take just 9 months until car #2 is completely paid off. That's impressive, but what is really powerful is what starts happening in month 10. Since you paid off Car #2, you have now recaptured its normal $491.08 monthly payment and it becomes part of your FP. So your FP is now $891.08. Just like a snowball rolling downhill, you will take your larger FP and roll it down to debt #2. The loan on Car #1 in this example, has a monthly payment of $671.90 and when added to your new $891.08 FP, the FP monthly payment on Car #1 will be a whopping $1562.98 every month. As you can see, in your debt payoff form, even though Car 1 has a $12,350 balance, it will be paid off in just 8 months. This is the power of my formula !

The growing FP from one debt to the next, to the next, until they are all gone. In most cases, people following the se-cret formula have completely eliminated all debt, except their mortgage in one to two years. They then frequently have an FP of 1.5 to 2 times their mortgage payment, or even more. This means they can often triple their mortgage payment every month. On the example that we provided, you will notice that the FP has grown to $2,060.97. By the time it cascades down to the $733.66 mortgage payment, it is nearly 3 times the regular mortgage payment. When they are added together, the FP monthly payment applied to the mortgage is $2,794.73 a month. Even though the mortgage has a $100,000 balance, it is gone in just 36 months. A mortgage that would have taken decades to pay off is now burning in the fireplace in just three years.

Don't forget, contact your mortgage holder directly and ask for specific instructions on how to make principle prepayments along with your regular monthly payment. When you begin paying your FP on your mortgage, your home equity will skyrocket for two reasons. One - 100% of your FP is reducing your principle balance. So your net worth, your wealth, is growing even as you pay off your debt. Two – the portion of your monthly payment that is interest will be falling dramatically each month because it is calculated on the remaining unpaid balance of the loan. Since your FP is pounding down this unpaid balance, the interest calculation will be performed each month on a smaller and smaller unpaid balance amount. More of your monthly payment amount will also be applied to the unpaid principle balance, accelerating the payoff process.

Important: As soon as you reduce the principle balance to less than 80% of the home's appraised value, check with the lender to be sure they are no longer charging you for PMI. This will eliminate the PMI monthly premium, lowering your monthly payment. This means that even more of your FP will be applied to your mortgage principle reduction.

Let's go back to our sample form and in column 7, you will be told the total number of months your debt elimination plan will take. Divide this number by 12 and you will know how many years it will take until you are completely debt free. In the example above, this family would be completely debt free in 72 months – exactly 6 years! This is approximately 24 years earlier than they would have taken to pay everything off it they had made the payments the way their creditors had them set up.

Now it's your turn

We have the blank form for you to calculate your FP and you will know how long it is going to take YOU to be debt free. You may want to make a couple of copies of the form before you start in case you want to try different scenarios later. Enter your FP at the top of the form and each debt, their balance and their monthly payment in the first three columns. From there it is addition and division. Follow the directions on the form and review the sample that we have prepared for you. Once you have completed the form you have a plan. You have the formula in your hands. This will take you out of debt, but you have to follow it.

Debt Free Form

Factor Prosperity

A. Write down your factor prosperity at right. $

B. Find your priority debt. This is the debt with the most take-home income:

C. Write down each debt's name in the first column below, its total balance in column 2, and its minimum monthly payments (excalading tax, insurance, or any amount you might typically add to it) in column 3.

C. Divide the total balance of each debt by ten monthly payment, and put the answer in column 4.

D. Prioritize your debts in column 5, beginning with the debt with the lowest division answer in column 4 as priority debt #1, the next lowest division answer as priority debt #2, and so on.

E. Column 6 is where you add your Accelerator Margin (from A, above) to the monthly payment amount for priority debt #1 and put this total in the right Accelerated Monthly Payment. Now divide the debt #1's Total Balance by this Accelerated Monthly Payment. The answer given in column 7.

F. When debt #1 is paid off, take its Accelerated Monthly Payment (which contains the original Accelerator Margin and debt #1's monthly payment) and add this amount to the monthly Payment of debt #2. Put the total in column 6 as debt #2's Accelerated Monthly Payment

G. (Continue adding each paid-off debt's Accelerated Monthly Payment to the monthly payment of the next priority debt to accelerate its payoff — until you've eliminated all your debts.

Name of Debt	Total Balance	Monthly Payment	Division Answer	Payoff Priority	Accelerated Monthly Payment	Months to Pay Off
1	2	3	4	5	6	7

H. Total Debt (total column 2):

I. Total Monthly Payments (total column 3): $

J. Total Accelerated Payments (A ÷ I): $

K. Years to debt-freedom (total columns 7 ÷ 12): $

Track Your Progress

You should track your progress every month against your DEBT FREE FORM . Use the UPDATING FP FORM to help you do just do that. Take it out and post it somewhere that you can see every day This will help you to avoid mistakes .If you know when a debt is suppose to be paid off and it's not you know you've been undisciplined and you cannot forget that discipline it is important part of our formula so use this form to help you in daly basis this way you will never going to lose track of your progress and will be debt free fast here the form

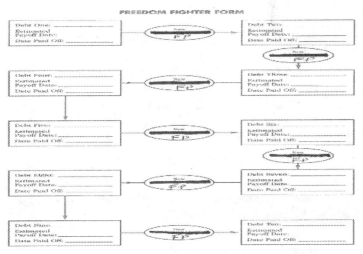

Now it's time to answers some question that you have in my experience here are some of questions that you are probably ask you self if you want to ask more questions please fell free to visit www.4001capitalmanagement.com

Question and Answers:

Question:
I don't have a mortgage. In fact, I've been saving up for a down payment. How does this apply to me?

Answer: If you're not yet making mortgage payments, you should use the formula to pay off all your credit debt (bank cards, store charge cards, gas cards with any balance on them, car loans). Once your debts are gone, put all the money you've freed up each month into a Money Market account or CD to more quickly build up a down payment for your home. As soon as you get into your new house, immediately start the process of paying off the mortgage using the the secret formula! Notice that we said pay off all your debts first...then begin saving for your down payment. This is the sequence that will get you in to your home the fastest. And it will improve your FICO score and your debt-to-income ratio.

Question: You mean I shouldn't be saving money all along?

Answer:
Every time you get conventional financial advice, it usually includes the instruction to build a little nest egg on the side while you work your way through life. Many will counsel you to save 10 percent of your income as an investment for the future. They call it "Pay yourself first." I agree with this principle, but not with where they tell you to invest it. If you're putting money into a savings or money market account at 1, 2, or 3 percent interest...or even government securities that generate 4 or 5 percent – while you are simultaneously

paying 15 percent or more on credit interest – you're moving backwards at a rate of at least nine to 13 percent a year. And when you compound that over years, it becomes a staggering loss of your wealth.

If you have any debt, the best, first investment of your money is to pay off that debt because you'll get an effective return on investment (ROI) equal to the interest rate that debt charges. So when I say "Pay yourself first," I mean pay the money toward debt-elimination. Save second. You'll be dollars ahead following this approach.

That's why I even recommend you consider temporarily suspending any savings you may doing right now, including deductions coming out of your paycheck at work, and add that monthly amount to your Accelerator Margin. You want to get as much of your income working on the debt pay-down as possible. Your money will do you a lot more good paying off 7 to 20 percent debt than it will earning 2 percent in a savings account.

Question: What about my 401(k)? Should I stop putting money into that?

Answer:
401(k) or 403(b) plans that you have at work are great retirement investment plans, because you're immediately earning your employer's contribution, and that can equal as much as 100 percent of your contribution. Plus, the growth of the total investment accumulates tax-deferred until you begin taking distributions in retirement. What I recommend is that you continue investing in your 401(k) or 403(b), but not a penny ore than your employer will match. Put all the rest into your Accelerator Margin until your debts are completely paid off – then raise your 401 (k) contribution to the maximum percentage of your pay that is allowed.

Question: But I am getting a really great tax deduction from my mortgage. Why would I want to give that up?

Answer:
Don't worry about the loss of your mortgage interest tax deduction or concern yourself with any other tax consequences. While you're paying off your mortgage, you're still getting your full tax deduction on the interest you pay.

Mortgage interest tax deduction is a losing proposition because you pay a dollar to your mortgage lender as interest and get back 25 to 40 cents from the government as a tax reduction. That's paying a dollar to get back 25 to 40 cents.

Question:
Why should I pay off my low interst rate mortgage when I could make so much more by investing in the market?

Answer:
On a typical monthly mortgage payment, 90 percent or more of the payment is interest each month. While the mortgage company made you feel like you were getting a 5 or 6 percent mortgage, you're actually paying 90+ percent of your money toward interest each month. It would only be 5 or 6 percent if you paid the entire balance off in the first year.

The other reason paying off your mortgage is a good idea is that paying off debt gibes you a guaranteed return on investment equal to the debt's interest rate, so you rmust only compare paying off your mortgage loan with investments that would also guarantee their return. What investments guarantee their returns? Growth/equity mutual funds do not guarantee their return. In fact, you can lose money in these funds. It's the same with individual stocks, bonds, real estate, precious metals, and almost all types of securities. The safest investments that do guarantee their return rates are U.S. Treasury instruments, such as bills, notes, and bonds. You'll find that long-term bonds generally offer the highest interest rate of the three, but this rate will always be less than current mortgage interest rates. So prepaying always gives you a higher return on your money than the best comparable, guaranteed-return investment.

We hope that you enjoy read this part of the book this is the formula this is it please apply have fun and don't forget give yourself a prize every time that you truly fell that you deserve you can make this dream be real in your life play as game and one more time you have any additional questions or comments please fell free to contact us at www.4001kcapitalmanagemt. com will be happy to help you .

PART 2

Twenty Tips to Never be in Debt Again and Build Prosperity

Our goal here is to keep you aware of the risk and temptation. Remember…. Never again will you be where you were, meaning, in debt. So, some of these tips must be done, no matter what. Others will be like a red light, things you will need to stop doing immediately. Also, these tips will allow you to get more involved with your financial life. Get a book, read a paper, watch a show! Hey – at the end, it's your money, your prosperity. Here we go…

Tip #1 –
Do not spend more than you make.

Do I need to further explain this? Keep your forms, track your expenses and make sure you don't go over your budget.

Tip#2 –
Do not use credit cards.

Remember what got you in debt in the first place?

Tip #3 –
If you don't have a 401k account – open one now

Make sure that you invest enough to maximize your employee match, if available. This is free money. Employers are giving money away and so is the government by offering tax-deferred savings. This is one way to build your prosperity.

Tip #4 –
Open an IRA (Investment Retirement Account)

After opening your 401k and making sure that you are putting away enough to get your employer's contribution, a great idea is to open an IRA account. Why? Because it offers the same tax benefits as an IRA, but here you can manage the account and buy, sell, and trade any stock or fund that you want with almost no restrictions. This is an amazing way to build your prosperity.

Tip #5 –
Build a 911 Fund.

The 911 Fund is to be built once you are debt free. This is simple. Its value should be equal to three months of paychecks. Remember you can use your Factor Prosperity to help you to build that fund.

Tip #6 –
Do not invest in Mutual Funds. Instead invest in ETF (Exchange Trade Funds).

Mutual funds are not bad, but they are charging you so many fees that you don't even know what you are paying. They are also complicated to trade. ETFs are traded like stocks and are almost free of any fees. So be smart, search and find out which one fits your investment style and stick with it. You will be introduced to some ETFs later.

Tip #7 –
Have a financial coach.

This is very important. Get someone who can help you to decide. It could be a friend, a teacher, or a professional. Just make sure that you understand what they are telling you and make the final decision for yourself.

Tip #8 –
Always have health insurance.

This is enemy number one against your prosperity. In America, this is one of the greatest factors causing bankruptcy and financial ruin. Protect yourself and always have health insurance.

Tip #9 –
Have life insurance.

If you have a family that depends on your income, there is no doubt that you should have life insurance. It will protect your wealth and your family in the case of your untimely demise.

Tip #10 –
Hold yourself accountable.

What does that mean? Respect your budget and your goal. If you did not do well this month, stop now, redirect, fix it and then move on in the right direction.

Tip #11 –
Determine how much you will spend month to month.

Again, you have to set your goal and stick with it. Sometimes you have a reason to spend more one month,. That's okay. But next month you need to get right back to the plan. Plan your work, and work your plan.

Tip #12 –
Plan your retirement.

This is a marathon, not a sprint. Get your 401k, IRAs and 911 Fund. Build your dream portfolio of dream stocks and keep focused on your goal.

Tip #13 –
Do not buy stocks and hold, buy and trade.

Be involved with the economic situation. The best stocks go down. For example, GE is in almost every 401k in America. In 2008, it dropped 78%. If it is time to sell, sell. Do not feel married to your stocks.

Tip #14 –
Do not ever, ever, ever invest your 401k money is your employer's stock options.

If you doubt the validity of this tip, talk to a former employee of Enron or Worldcom. By investing your retirement funds in your current employer you are taking a huge risk. One you don't want to take.

Tip #15 –
Always roll over your 401k into an IRA.

Let's say you work for Target and leave to work at Apple, instead of leaving your money with your old employer or rolling it over to your new 401k, just transfer it to your IRA. Don't forget you will have your same tax shelter and now with your new IRA, you will be able to manage it yourself and buy and sell with no restrictions.

Tip #16 –
Watch TV.

Yes, watch TV. I'm not saying you should decide what to buy or sell based on what your see on MSNBC, but Fox News, ABC and Bloomberg all have shows that can help to educate you. Here are some that I recommend: Mad Money, On the Money, The Suze Orman Show, The Kublow Report. All of these offer different perspectives and information for you. Knowledge is learning. Become a lifelong learner.

Tip #17 –
Create your portfolio of stocks.

Let's call it your portfolio of dreams. Now you have no debt, you are investing in your 401k and your IRA, and you have built your 911 Fund. Now it's time to build your Speculative Portfolio. Please do it. This will be discussed in the next part.

Tip #18 –
Teach your kids about the stock market.

This is a marathon – not a sprint – it's about prosperity and how nice to give your child the tools they need to succeed financially in life. Instead of starting a savings account, get them a broker investment account. Don't worry if he is 5, 10 or 15 years old. Get him involved with the stock market. Buy one share of the things that he loves – Disney, Viacom, McDonald's and Nintendo. This way you can play while teaching him to build his own prosperity.

Tip #19 –
Do not worry about taxes.

I know – no one likes to pay taxes, but don't base your decision to buy or sell stocks based on the tax season. Many people lost money because of this theory. Sell if you have to. Pay the tax. Remember…. We buy and trade. Not buy and hold.

Tip #20 –
Be Diversified!

You can't put all your eggs in one basket. Study the sectors and industries that you want to invest in. Diversification means not buying Exxon and Chevron in the same portfolio. If you want to invest in fossil fuels, you need to look into green options and oil, or electric and coal.

Conclusions:

I hope that you understand that by following these tips you are on the right path. Now you can deepen your understanding. Do a personal search and do a great job for yourself by building your prosperity and a phenomenal future for you and your family.

PART 3

Meet and Potatoes

My goal here is not get you load up with information that you don't even know you bought this book to be debt free, right ?However, what you gonna do with your money after you free ? Again my goal in this part is make you curious ! Because if you get curious you will go after more information more knowledge and this is where the magic show in your life knowledge+ information =success and prosperity ! This is a great equation ! I hope that you get really hungry for more knowledge and information, you apply this equation into your trade or investment and you will make a lot of money.. Ok having sad that I wanna start with 5 mistakes that a lot of people make and you have to avoid, here it is:

1 – Buying stock because it looks cheap - The share price of stock should not be determining factor when you're buying stocks . A$5stock is no cheaper than a $15 stock. If both stocks goup15% you gain the same percentage in both stocks(works same way with losses also)

2 – Falling in love with stock - Too many investors fall in love with stock and refuse to close out of it even when the writing is on the wall. A stock should be treated as an investment and if that investment turns sour, one should get out of it as fast as possible. Just remember no stock remains a hot stock to buy forever.

3 – Following the masses - All too often a person would just buy a hot stock because they see everyone else buying and feel that it cannot go down. This type of investor often

ends up being "bag holder". They are left holding the bag when the stock turns sour and the prices drops.

4 – Spam Messages-Buying stocks from email that you received recommending the stock is one of the worse way to invest. Usually these stocks are penny stocks that have little or no value and will end up going belly up at some point. Do not buy stock from spam period.

5 – Buying stocks without due diligence - Buying the next hot stock requires you do proper diligence, or it can be a flop that leads to loss. It's a good idea to get tips from sites like thestreet.com,vectorvest.com,esignal.com and so on and most important that you do your own diligence prior your purchase.

Well , just those informations will help you and save a lot of money, please read again and apply when you are to invest or trade.

ETF

In the begining of this book I sad buy ETF don't buy mutual funds and here I will give you 5 reason why you should buy ETF , in my opnion for ordinary amercans ETF is simple is waht you see is what you get ! no hide fee , no comision , no need to pay manager so just that would be so easy to do deal but here reason number

1 – ETFs Cost Less. Even though you do not receive a bill from mutual fund providers, you are charged a fee through the expense ratio. This is the primary way in which your fund family makes money. The typical mutual fund will run you 1.4%, or $1400 on every $100,000 that you invest. The average ETF has been estimated at approximately 0.36%. Even rounding up to 0.4%... $400 on every $100,000 invested is a lot less expensive than $1400

2 – ETFs Track Indexes...And Indexing Beats Actively Managed Mutual Funds. It may represent Wall Street's dirtiest secret, but fund managers do not beat pre-established indexes over significant lengths of time. Over any 10-year period studied, the overwhelming majority of actively managed mutual funds with overcompensated stock-picking gurus cannot keep up with the benchmarks (a.k.a. indexes) that they are paid to beat. When a few managers do outperform, the stock picker has often taken excessive risks in one segment of the economy (e.g., technology, energy, etc.). Yet given time, those big risks come back to bite. In short, ETFs track indexes, and indexing are your preferred road to success.

3 – Pricing. Traditional mutual funds are priced at the end of the day. you have no control over the price you purchase at and, more importantly the price you may wish to sell at. In contrast, like individual stocks, ETFs makes it possible for you to choose the price point you wish to buy at. And, should you need to sell to protect your portfolio from sharp downturns, you have control over the price you wish to sell at as well.

4 – Tax Efficiency. Traditional mutual funds buy and sell stocks. And many active managers have turnover rates... rates of turning over a portfolio in a year... of 100%. That's a lot of buying and selling of stock picks. The mutual fund structure. passes along capital gains form the buying and selling activity to the fund shareholder. You may not have any personal gains from being a fund shareholder, but come year-end, you are likely to experience a distribution that you must pay tax on... even when you are simply holding the fund! ETFs have next-to-no turnover because indexes rarely change. The low turnover of ETFs leads limit capital gains distributions and, due to a unique structure for ETFs, even rebalanced indexes do not necessarily have to buy and sell. In short, if you wish to keep the money you make, rather than pay taxes, ETFs win hands down!

5 – Transparency. When you buy a mutual fund, what do you really know about it? You see a few stars from a rating group like Morningstar. You see a number of calendar year percentage gains. Do you really know what the fund manager invests in? You may get as description of the top 10 holdings in a previous 3 month period, but you are essentially, guessing. In contrast, an exchange-traded fund (ETF) represents a specific index. You know exactly the stocks in that index and exactly the weight of each stock in the index. That transparency gives you the confidence to know what you are investing in...precisely.

Do you need more ? Please instead buy mutual funds just buy ETF !

You need a coach

Guys you think Warren Buffett decide wich stock he is gonna buy or sale by himself ? No ! He has a time , people that working together to help him to make the best decision. We need a coach , we need a help not to decide for us but to guide m, to show the options that we have with that in mind here how you should pick your coach:

Experience. How long has the individual been coaching? While there are six-week courses for those who wish to become a financial coach, this does not necessarily guarantee that they have established expertise in the area most important to you. Look for a coach who has had extensive training for at least two years, followed by multiple exams showing his or her competence in the area. A certified _financial planner_ and a certified public accountant both meet these criteria. Additionally, you need to know how long the coach has been practicing in that particular field. Also, providing any and all licenses is proof that the individual is engaged in ongoing education, as well.

Compensation. How much does the financial coach charge and on what basis are the fees incurred? Also, who provides payment for his or her services? For instance, does the coach work for a _bank_ or other financial institution and receive commissions from it?

Personality. You'll probably be able to tell within the first five minutes of interviewing a perspective financial coach if he or she is suitable for your needs. You may think that personality should not be a factor, but if you clearly don't get along with your coach it may cause problems later on. This is because one of the basic tenets of hiring a financial coach is trust and confidence that he or she will do the job you hired them to do. As long as you're comfortable with the coach and can confide in and depend upon them to guide you into a successful financial future, then you've found someone quite special.

Professionalism. Does the financial coach conduct business in a courteous and professional manner? Does he or she set appointments well in advance and arrive on time? Are your questions and concerns addressed immediately or, at least, in a timely manner? You wouldn't expect any less from your family doctor, so why would you settle for someone who doesn't offer the same level of professionalism in the financial world?

Expertise. Whether you're hiring a coach to help with _retirement planning_, tuition for your children's college education, _investments_, _insurance_ or _starting a new business_, you undoubtedly want someone that has expertise in a specific niche. Ideally, of course, you'd want a financial coach who's proficient in all of these areas.

Just as you would take the time and effort to find the right doctor, lawyer or baby-sitter, use the same diligence to articulate your needs in finding the best financial coach available. Finding someone who understands your financial vision and can draw on practical experience to help you achieve it is even better than finding lost money.

Now you have almost everything right ? I wanna say that I recommend you buy the books that I mesion at the end of this book , If you have anymore questions just write to us, and we will be glad to help you even recommend more books if you want to or need to .But I could not end this part without give you the real meet and potatoes for you to trade or invest , I am not saying to you to buy tomorrow without study the season that we are , we already cover this part but these names that I am giving to you, it is gonna make money in the long run just one thing invest your money it is a marathon not a sprint so thinks about that all right ? So here the meet in potatoes ,G OOG,AAPL,RIMM,AMZN,PBR,GS,PEP,TRN,EBAY and the best ETF DVY Again if you wanna know more about those , Well you will have to study and find out why they are market movers and make a lot of money for me and a lot of my clients .Now even if you have a portfolio I don't want you close your eyes what I mean by that ? Hey time to, sell ? Sell it ! So those rules are for investor and trades, and I find them very helpful in the daily bases again I want to remind you my goal is opening your mind make you curious and if you ask yourself why for each rule here and if you do that you will learn more and more , This Book has a goal to make you debt free and after that get you ready to invest and here are my rules Let's say King's rules.

1 – Sell the losers and let the winners run.
2 – It's better to average up than to average down.
3 – Buy high and sell higher
4 – Learn how to make money in a down market
5 – Learn how to trade options
6 – Have a wachtlist of stocks that are marketmovers like GOOG,IBM,AA,AAPLA,GS , and so on.
7 – Use stop losses always !
8 – Good company buys their own stock.
9 – Stay away from penny stock
10 – Heavy volume prices rises , light volume prices fall.

Now if you have 1000 questions this is just great means, I did my job well ,when we have questions in our mind, we are ready to learn , and now I believe you are ! I hope that you really feel hungry for more informations and knowledge go out there find the best books , audio books and learn as much you can you can beat the market, and you can make a lot of money , In my opnion there is no place that you can make more money than in the stock market , I hope that you enjoy this chapter as much, I enjoy writing !

Good luck in your investments !

PART 4

Bibliography

Here we will review the secret of the secret formula. My frustration and why not say sadness brought me to the point where I wanted to do something to help people to get out of debt, improve their life and make their dreams come true.

I hope after you read this you truly set your mind for a new beginning. What I did was I went deep inside brilliant minds and put a lot of what they said in their books here for you. I want to thank all of them and give them the credit because without them and their brilliant minds, I would never been able to do this book. If you want to go deeper into their brilliant minds and know how I built this secret formula. Here is the secret of the secret.

Go online:
www.tonyrobbins.com
www.gettheedge.com
www.personalpower.com

Find out how brilliant Tony and his program are.

You have to read Jim Cramer's **Stay Mad for Life**. He is intelligent, successful and his knowledge is beyond our imagination. He put together an awesome plan for your retirement.

Suze Orman has **Action Plan 2009**. Who does not need a financial coach like

Suze? She cares and speaks our language. She is brilliant and her success is because she deeply cares about those that need her help.

If you want to be successful in the stock market, read **How to Make Money in the Stock Market, but William J.**

O'Neill. He is an icon in this business and he has created a formula that if followed could lead to millions.

Transforming Debt into Wealth System was written by John Cummuta, a guy who was at one point in deep debt. He turned himself around and wrote this program that helps to transform and improve people's lives.

Lastly is the **Secret to Attracting Money** by Joe Vitale. You are now free of debt and have a better life, or are at least going in that direction. Feed yourself with good things, books, music and movies. Dr. Vitale put together this audio and workbook that is a gift to people who have turned their lives around. You can also go to www.mrfire.com and learn more about this program. Now you know the secret of the secret formula. Why don't you jump on this bibliography and delve deeper than you ever dreamed of being and learn more of the secrets to be rich, successful and mind free.

Bonus:

This is the most amazing and exciting help and guidance that you can get. I know the secret formula is simple and easy, but if you feel that you need extra help, go to www.4001kmanagment.com and get help. You can get a financial coach that will work with you and design a formula just for you. The results will make you debt free, but will also change your mind with their four-hour program. Invest in the financial coaching program and become not just debt-free, but build financial prosperity and a comfortable retirement

Final Thoughts:

In life we all have moments that make us stop and think deep inside. One day I was walking in a little coffee shop and I heard two men saying that the world changed so much. Now everybody is in debt, including his son. He expressed great worry about the son's lifestyle and the way that his son was living. At that moment I thought, "I think he is right." And realized that even I wasn't living a prosperous life. I asked myself, "What can I do to help myself and others?" That is when I began my research and found this very helpful formula to help you achieve prosperity. Now I want to share with you some final thoughts. Here they are:

1 – Never give up!
Almost nothing works the first time it is attempted, just because what you are doing doesn't seem to be working, it just means that it may not be working right now. If it was easy, everyone would be doing it and you wouldn't have the opportunity.

2 – When you are ready to quit, you are closer than you think.
There is an old Chinese saying, "The temptation to quit will be greatest just before you are about to succeed."

3 – Focus on what you want to have happen.
Remember, "As you think, so shall you be."

4 – Take things one day at a time.
No matter how difficult your situation, if you can get through. Don't look too far into the future, focus on the present moment, and you can get through anything one day at a time.

5 – Measure everything of significance.
Anything that is measured and watched will improve.

6 – There is always a reason to smile. Find it –
after all you are lucky to be alive. Life is too short. My brother always reminded me that we are not here for a long time, just a good time.

Let's summarize,

Here are some of the things that I have learned while building financial independence.

I need a financial independence plan. I went through a lot of difficult financial times to learn this formula. Why not learn from my mistakes, instead of experiencing this yourself. I had to get out of debt, completely out of debt, so I would own everything in my life and no longer worry about money. That way I could put nearly all of my income to work, to earn interest, and build retirement wealth. I knew I would never be able to stop working if I didn't do this.

I had to take action, change the day-to-day operations of my life. I learned that the path I was on, the same path as the other 95 percent of Americans leads to financial doom. Look around you and if you are living your life like most of the people around you, you are in that group.

I was going to attempt a home based business of my own, I wanted a business that would product residual to cumulative income and I wanted a business I would enjoy doing everyday.

I needed to be willing to pay the price of success in advance. I had to be willing to work at it. I had to learn to sacrifice TV or other recreation time to get it done. I needed a long-term vision.

I needed to ignore the short-term pain in order to be able to achieve the long-term gain. I need to learn to delay gratification. I couldn't buy everything I wanted the minute I wanted it.

Don't wait! Don't sit around thinking about it – do it. What would your day be like if you didn't have to think about where the next dollar is coming from? That is true independence and you deserve to enjoy it.

I hope that the principles I have shared with you here are helpful to your life. They are as true and real as the laws of gravity. I have learned many of them the tough way. I hope you will learn them the easy way.

Good luck and God bless you in your journey.